RL:38

D1119980

In My Neighborhood

GARBAGE COLLECTORS

Many thanks to the garbage collectors of North York

P.B. and K.L.

First U.S. edition 1998

12/2000 J fund 15⁰⁰

Text copyright © 1991 by Paulette Bourgeois
Illustrations copyright © 1991 by Kim LaFave

Published in Canada by   Published in the U.S. by
Kids Can Press Ltd.   Kids Can Press Ltd.
29 Birch Avenue   4500 Witmer Industrial Estates
Toronto, ON, M4V 1E2   Niagara Falls, NY 14305-1386

Designed by N.R. Jackson
Typeset by Cybergraphics Co. Inc.
Printed in Hong Kong by Everbest Company Limited

US   98 0 9 8 7 6 5 4 3 2
US PA   00 0 9 8 7 6 5 4 3 2 1

Canadian Cataloguing in Publication Data
Bourgeois, Paulette
    Garbage collectors

(In my neighborhood)
ISBN 1-55074-440-2 (bound)   ISBN 1-55074-826-2 (pbk.)

1. Refuse and refuse disposal — Juvenile literature.
2. Refuse collectors — Juvenile literature.   I. LaFave, Kim.
II. Title.   III. Series: Bourgeois, Paulette. In my
neighborhood.

TD792.B68 2000   j362.72'8   C97-931105-5

Kids Can Press is a Nelvana company

In My Neighborhood

GARBAGE COLLECTORS

Paulette Bourgeois

Kim LaFave

KIDS CAN PRESS

A garbage truck rounds the corner. It stops and starts. The brakes screech. Sam, the garbage collector, who is sometimes called a sanitation worker or sanitation engineer, runs back and forth, back and forth. Today, he'll walk 15 miles and hardly go anywhere. The garbage is heavy. And there's lots of it. In one year, every family throws out 200 big bags of trash.

"Hey, Sam," calls Mabel, the truck driver. "I wonder where Mrs. Green is going in such a hurry."

Sam wears a bright vest so that drivers can see him from far away.

Mabel squeezes the truck between parked cars. The children run toward it. Mabel shouts, "Please stay back!" She doesn't want them to get hurt by the truck.

"Is this a stinky job?" the children ask.

Sam laughs. "Only in the beginning. Now I'm used
to it. But it can be messy. Sometimes the bags leak."
"Yuck," say the children. But Sam doesn't mind. He
does an important job. Besides, he keeps clean clothes
in the truck in case he has to change.

One of the biggest garbage cans in the world is inside the garbage truck. A garbage truck holds more than five tons of crushed garbage bags. All that garbage weighs as much as an African elephant!

Sam tosses the bags into the hopper at the back of the garbage truck.

The truck keeps moving. It will stop at
500 houses today.
   "Hey, Mabel, I think Mrs. Green has
taken up jogging."

There's hardly any garbage in front of Mark's house. That's because Mark's family follows the three R's: Reduce, Reuse and Recycle.

They use their bags and containers over and over again.

They complain to company presidents and store owners when there is too much cardboard, plastic and paper packaging around food and toys.

They use lunch boxes and thermoses instead of bags and juice boxes.

They buy at bulk food stores.

They use cloth bags instead of paper or plastic.

They put newspapers, cans and clear glass in a recycling box.

They put leaves, vegetable peels, dead flowers, cut grass, egg shells, coffee grounds and tea bags into their composter.

A special truck picks up garbage that can be used again. Newspapers go in one bin. Clear glass goes in another bin. Cans go in another bin. Some plastic containers and some papers cannot be recycled.

"Whoops!" says the collector, throwing out a green glass bottle.

Garbage that can be recycled goes to factories where it is made into other things. Glass can be ground up and used to make roads. Old newspaper is turned into cardboard or shingles for roofs. Cans are melted and made into new cans.

Some garbage is too dangerous for regular pickup.
It's taken to hazardous waste centers where experts
make sure it is buried or reused safely. Some cities
have trucks to pick up hazardous waste from homes.
Hazardous waste should never be put out with regular
garbage.

Drain cleaners, oil paints, paint thinner, batteries
and polish for metal and furniture are all hazardous
waste.

"Hey, Sam," says Mabel. "That Mrs. Green sure is friendly. She keeps waving at you."

Sam piles the garbage bags into the truck. Whenever the hopper is full, Sam pulls the lever on the side of the truck. It signals a wide metal blade to move down and crush the garbage. "GRRRRRRRRRRRR," it growls. Then the blade scoops the compacted garbage into the belly of the truck.

Just as Sam is about to pull the lever, Mrs. Green catches up. She is panting and puffing. "Stop!" she gasps. Mrs. Green whispers something to Sam.

Together they rip open the bags in the hopper. There, nestled between the chicken bones and the tea bags, are Mrs. Green's false teeth.

When Mabel's truck is full, she drives to the top level of a transfer station. Mabel pushes a lever, and the garbage empties out of her truck. A bulldozer squishes the garbage and shoves it through a hole in the floor into the waiting tractor-trailer that will go to the landfill site.

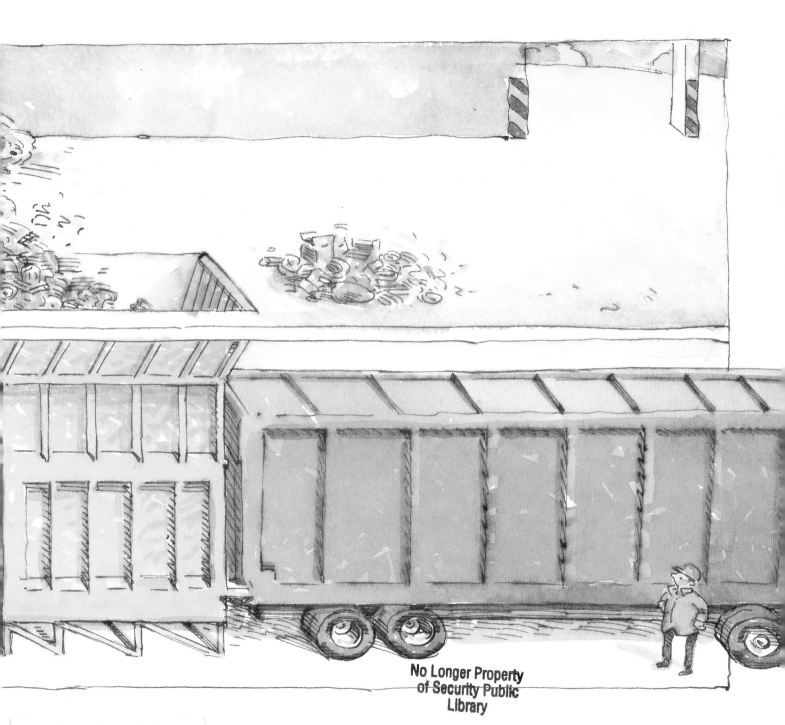

Most garbage is dumped into a hole in the ground at a landfill site. A bulldozer buries it. The garbage dump grows higher and higher until it becomes a garbage mountain. One day, there will be no more space to bury garbage.

In some places, garbage is burned in an open pit or in an incinerator. Some people think that the smoke from burning garbage hurts plants and air and water.

In the country, people take their garbage to the dump themselves. Sometimes they come home with something that another person has thrown out. As Mabel always says, "One person's garbage is somebody else's treasure."

At apartment buildings, the garbage is stored in gigantic containers. A special garbage truck with metal arms picks up each container and empties it.

Some sanitation workers collect trash in the parks.

Others collect the litter off the streets and sidewalks.

Even at night, garbage trucks prowl the quiet city streets, picking up garbage from stores, office buildings and factories. Tonight the garbage collectors are lucky.

"Look at this. A box of toy cars without wheels."
"Look here. My kids could build something with these."
The garbage collectors are allowed to keep every-
thing they find.

But garbage collectors don't always keep what they find. Just ask Sam and Mabel!